Brian Webb & Peyton Skipwith

John Piper
DESIGN

Antique Collectors' Club

Design series format by Brian Webb
Design, John Piper © 2013 Brian Webb & Peyton Skipwith
All images © Estate of John Piper 2013 and reproduced with their kind permission

Grateful thanks to Hugh Fowler-Wright for the many images specially photographed
for this book by George Richards

World copyright reserved

ISBN 978-1-85149-728-7

British Library Cataloguing-in-Publication data
A catalogue record for this book is available from the British Library.

Antique Collectors' Club
Sandy Lane, Old Martlesham,
Woodbridge, Suffolk IP12 4SD, UK
Tel: 01394 389950 Fax: 01394 389999
Email: info@antique-acc.com
or
ACC Distribution,
6 West, 18th Street, Suite 4B,
New York, NY 10011, USA
Tel: 212 645 1111 Fax: 212 989 3205
Email: sales@antiquecc.com
www.antiquecollectorsclub.com

The cover design is reproduced from Prometheus by Edwin Muir, Ariel Poem,
Faber and Faber 1954
Endpapers are reproduced from the Faber & Faber Christmas Card, 1951
Opposite, Prometheus by Edwin Muir, 1954

Published by Antique Collectors' Club, Woodbridge, England
Design by Webb & Webb Design Limited, London
Printed and bound in China

Invention in Colour, *auto-lithograph from collaged original,* Signature 6, *July 1937.* Signature, *the magazine of fine printing and book arts, was edited by Oliver Simon and printed by the Curwen Press before and after World War Two.*

Design
John Piper

John Piper remains something of an enigma: an antiquarian who
was among the pioneers of non-representational art in Britain;
an abstract painter who drew his inspiration from the paintings
of Turner and mediaeval stained glass; and a romantic with a
penchant for geometric design. At heart he was a mediaevalist, a
dedicated church-crawler, who read the historic layers of ancient
monuments and buildings like so many palimpsests; or, as with
Stonehenge, 'like a slowly evolving animal.'[1] Buildings and
landscape to him were living, vital, elements – he loved what in
Romney Marsh he described as their 'look of having been used and
almost over-used by man'. At the same time, abstraction was an
intellectual exercise; as he wrote to Paul Nash: 'classical exercises
and the "discipline" of abstraction open a road to one's heart – but
they are not the heart itself',[2] later telling Richard Ingrams that
while, during the 1930s, he had taken the abstract practice very
seriously, he 'never had any intention of remaining an abstract
artist'.[3]

Like Claud Lovat Fraser, one of his earliest heroes and exemplars,
he had to serve an apprenticeship in his father's law practice before
being able to shed the yoke and free himself to pursue the career of
his choice. Although he was diligent in his law studies, like Fraser,
he could not resist the temptation to make sketches from the office
window. In formal terms, he came late to art and, although he had
considerably more professional training than Lovat Fraser, he was
always to remain something of an autodidact.

John Egerton Christmas Piper was born on the 13th December
1903: that extraordinary year for British art which witnessed the
births of Eric Ravilious, Edward Bawden, Richard Eurich, Barbara
Hepworth, Ceri Richards, Tom Hennell and Graham Sutherland.
His father, Charles Alfred Piper, a partner in Piper, Smith & Piper,
a firm of London solicitors, prided himself on being a professional

man with a broad interest in culture. In 1910, he demolished the mid-1860s Italianate villa in Epsom, where John had been born, replacing it with an up-to-date neo-Georgian house; he attended art classes, wrote an autobiography and encouraged his son's antiquarian interests, taking him in the early 'twenties on a tour of Northern Italy.[4] John worked out their itinerary basing it on Joseph Pennell's *The Road in Tuscany*, giving them time to study Venice, Siena, Volterra and San Gimignano. Throughout his life, Piper liked to have precedents and documentation. Part of Charles's intent in undertaking this trip was to impress on his son the advantages in life available to the successful professional man, in the hope that this might reconcile him to the law and divert him from his desire to pursue the precarious life of an artist. Once enrolled as an articled clerk in the Vincent Square offices of Messrs Piper, Smith & Piper, he was to remain there for close on five years. The one redeeming feature for him of this unwelcome imposition was the fact that Vincent Square was within easy walking distance of the Tate and National Galleries, where he could usefully employ his lunch hours. Also on errands to the Law Courts he was able to drop in on his friend Miles Marshall at the old-fashioned printing works in Milford Lane, just off the Strand. There, as Piper later recalled, they would 'talk about type faces and type books, look at all the lovely paper and card samples, watch things coming off the machines and smell the pervasive printer's ink.'[5]

As a boy, John had shown an early predilection for church visiting, a passion that was to remain with him throughout his life; a tab dated 8th March 1916 in his Surrey edition of Morris's *County Churches*, records that he had already visited sixty-six of them: remarkable dedication for a twelve-year-old. By the time he was sixteen, he was secretary of the Surrey Archaeological Society, and making schematic drawings of churches in the manner of F.L.Griggs's illustrations to the various volumes of Macmillan's *Highways and Byways* county guides. These, and other county and church guides were his constant companions on his long, discursive and carefully plotted bicycle rides. In due course, bicycles were superseded by motor cars, but this pattern of journeys with frequent diversions, designed to take in as many places and buildings of interest as possible, was to remain an important ingredient of his life; he would often be accompanied by his wife, Myfanwy, John Betjeman or J.M.'Jim' Richards, by then editor of *Architectural Review*.

Piper's eldest brother, Charles, was killed in 1915 at the second battle of Ypres; a traumatic loss that probably strengthened his father's resolve that John should join the family firm. John, however, while submitting to his father's wishes, remained as determined as ever to expand his artistic interests and practice and assert his own personality. He had initially been encouraged in this endeavour by John Hilton, a sociologist friend of his father's, who had an interest in literature and modern art. Hilton's influence was later augmented, and largely superseded, by that of Victor Kenna, a young clergyman recently demobilised from the Marines, who came as a curate to St Martin's, Epsom, the Pipers' local church. He was a man of wide erudition, interested in architecture, archaeology, prehistoric art and contemporary painting, as well as music, having studied with Artur Schnabel. Kenna took Piper's education in hand, transforming his boyhood enthusiasms into something more disciplined and scholarly, laying the foundations for his later work on the County *Guides*, Britten's operas and ecclesiastical stained glass. Many years later, Piper wrote of his 'old clergyman friend… who had an important and lasting influence on my life, combining as he did (and alas so few other clergyman do) an understanding of the authority of the church and the authority of form in paintings and sculpture.'[6] With Kenna's encouragement, he read and studied enthusiastically, enjoying the 1918 Diaghilev season, responding particularly to Picasso's designs for *The Three Cornered Hat* and *Parade*, as well as Derain's *La Boutique Fantasque*, and revelling in the Tate Gallery's exhibition of William Blake's illustrations to Dante's *The Divine Comedy*, prior to their dispersal.

With boyish enthusiasm Piper took to annotating his books, often noting the date of purchase: Hilaire Belloc's *The Stane Street* (1919); *Georges Rouault* (1920) in the Gallimard series *Les Peintres* Français *Nouveaux*; Hippisley Cox's *The Green Roads of England* (February 27th, 1921), and so on. With Ulric Daubeny's *Ancient Cotswold Churches* – purchased July 2nd 1921 – he went even further, drawing a map of the region, the better to enable him to devise a comprehensive bicycle tour, and making an index of the illustrations. Regrettably, he did not date his copy of Claud Lovat Fraser's *Poems from the early*

BOOKMARK

JOHN PIPER
23.

IN petticoat of green,
Her hair about her eyne,
Phillis, beneath an oak,
Sat milking her fair flock.
'Mongst that sweet-strained moisture,
rare delight!
Her hand seem'd milk, in milk it was so white.
WILLIAM DRUMMOND.

32

I FEED a flame within, which so torments me,
That it both pains my heart, and yet contents me:
'Tis such a pleasing smart, and I so love it,
That I had rather die than once remove it.

Yet he for whom I grieve shall never know it:
My tongue does not betray, nor my eyes show it.
Not a sigh, not a tear, my pain discloses,
But they fall silently, like dew on roses.

Thus, to prevent my love from being cruel,
My heart's the sacrifice, as 'tis the fuel:
And while I suffer this to give him quiet,
My faith rewards my love, though he deny it.

On his eyes will I gaze, and there delight me;
Where I conceal my love no frown can fright me:
To be more happy, I dare not aspire;
Nor can I fall more low, mounting no higher.
DRYDEN.

33

JOHN PIPER,
ALRESFORD,
EPSOM

John Piper's copy of The Lute of Love, *a small anthology of poems illustrated by Claud Lovat Fraser, published by Selwyn and Blount and inscribed by Piper in 1923, the year in which he produced his Lovat Fraser-influenced bookmark.*

works of Charles Cotton, but he is likely to have acquired it shortly after its publication in 1922; the vignette of a cottage among trees on Piper's printed bookmark the following year is a direct pastiche of Fraser's illustrations, as are his designs for the title pages of his two little books of poems – *Wind in the Trees* and *The Gaudy Saint and Other Poems* – as well as in his father's *Sixty-three: Not Out*, which, like the Charles Cotton, was printed at the Curwen Press. Despite the absence of formal training at this period, it is clear that he was seeking exemplars and modelling his work on theirs: the influence of Frank Brangwyn's loose wash-drawings in Indian ink, especially those of windmills, is also evident in some of these illustrations.

Although Piper held fast to his intention to become an artist, he had to bow to parental pressure and join Piper, Smith and & Piper; however his failure to pass the Law Society Examinations four years later, created an impasse that was only resolved by his father's death in March 1927. He left the firm with relief and immediately tried to enrol at the Royal College of Art. He was, however, first sent by Hubert Wellington, the registrar, to Richmond School of Art to improve his life drawing under the supervision of Raymond Coxon, before finally being admitted to the College that September. Although he was now firmly on the road to achieving his ambition, things were not totally straight forward. As Morris Kestelman, one of his tutors, recorded: 'We saw that he knew what he wanted to do, and had a pretty good idea of the way to do it – there wasn't much more we could do than leave him alone to get on with his drawing – he was nearly four years older than the average student when he came to the College, and he felt it – there was an awkwardness in his drawing that came from lack of practice – you could see that he had the vision, but he hadn't the manual dexterity to get his idea pinned down.'[7]

After the frustration of his years studying law, Piper was in a hurry; he was dismissive of the painting school at the College, finding the design school more stimulating, especially the work being done in stained glass and lithography by Francis Spear. Piper was eager to put his name before the public, exhibiting several woodcuts at the Arlington Gallery the year he entered the College; the principal, William Rothenstein characterised these as being 'Nashey and Whitey' – not bad rôle models, as Paul Nash and Ethelbert White

were two of the leading practitioners in the medium; he also went
to the Tate Gallery to copy Cézanne's *A Rocky Landscape Aix*, which
was on loan from the Samuel Courtauld Trust. Whilst working on
this, he met H.S. 'Jim' Ede, then an assistant at the Gallery. As a
result of Kenna's enthusiasm for primitive sculpture, and his own
study of Turner's paintings, Piper had developed an awareness
of abstract form; it was probably this underlying appreciation
of what Cézanne was seeking in the rocks at Aix that impressed
Ede, who became a friend and, in due course, introduced him to
Braque at a dinner along with Ben Nicholson, Barbara Hepworth
and Jean Hélion. Hearing that Picasso was to exhibit a collection
of *papiers collés* at the Galerie Pierre the following year – 1935 – he
immediately planned a trip to Paris.[8]

Piper's impatience with the Royal College was compounded
by his desire to marry Eileen Holding, whom he had met at
Richmond School of Art; on discovering that marriage was firmly
discouraged by the authorities, he tendered his resignation and left
without taking his diploma. The couple settled in St Peter's Square,
Hammersmith, and also, for a while, at the cottage at Betchworth
in Surrey that his mother gave him, and which had been specially
built by Eden and Joseph Henry "Socrates" Woodger. Woodger,
the Professor of Philosophy at the University of London – hence
his nickname – had inherited a considerable fortune from his
grandfather who had pioneered the first commercial kipper-
smoking process. The Woodgers befriended the young Piper and,
like Kenna, were keen to foster and guide his talents, which now
found a further outlet through writing. His first review for *The
Nation and Athenaeum*, devoted to the Royal Society of Arts' industrial
design competition appeared in August 1929. Over the next few
years he was to contribute reviews on a range of subjects covering
art, music, theatre and film.

In 1930, the Surrey Archaeological Society published A.V. Peatling's
Ancient Stained and Painted Glass in the Churches of Surrey, a copy of which
Piper acquired the following year. Among its many illustrations,
it included the 13th-century window at West Horsley depicting
the martyrdom of St Catherine, which was to become almost a
talisman for Piper, and of which he made a fine copy. Mediaeval
stained glass was one of his most enduring passions, as well as

In 1936 Piper made a watercolour copy of the medieval Waterperry 'Christ in Majesty' window. The painting was exhibited at Chichester Cathedral in 1944, Piper's reasoning was 'to illustrate the great traditions of English Church art and at the same time encourage contemporary work in preparation for the rebuilding of churches after the war'.

an essential key to abstraction. The slabs of glass, the leading and the richness of colour of these windows, whether in small parish churches – such as West Horsley; Arlingham, Gloucestershire; Waterperry, Oxon; and Grateley in Hampshire – or in the vastness of the Cathedral at Chartres, were to provide a fundamental source of inspiration not only for his paintings and designs for stained glass, both figurative and abstract, but also for work in other media. As a young man, Piper had made a copy of the 13th-century 'Stoning of St Stephen' window at Grateley, which had been relocated from Salisbury Cathedral in 1815. He wrote later that he had 'learnt more about using colours doing this copy than I have ever learned before or since.'[9] What he learnt about the use of colour was undoubtedly important, but perhaps even more so was the connection it established for him with the distant past, which was to become an essential component of his modernism; a fact emphasised by the reproduction of this copy in *Axis 7*.

By the early 1930s, he was in command of virtually the entire aesthetic vocabulary that was to last him throughout his life, as well as the technical means with which to express it. Only one key element was missing, and this was provided on a June evening in 1934 when, staying with Ivon Hitchens at Sizewell in Suffolk, he was asked by his host to go to the station at Saxmundham to meet a fellow-guest, Myfanwy Evans. Myfanwy had already encountered Piper in print through her English tutor at Oxford, Edmund Blunden, who had taken over the editorship of the renamed *New Statesman and Nation*. An immediate rapport was established between them and the following month Myfanwy went to Paris armed with an introduction from Piper to Jean Hélion: by the time she returned to England she had been charged to start a publication devoted to abstract art along the lines of the French publication *Abstraction-Création*. This was the genesis of *Axis*, the first issue of which, with a cover designed by Piper, appeared in January 1935 priced at two shillings and sixpence. Piper's marriage was already breaking up; Eileen eloped with their Hammersmith neighbour Ceri Richards, while John and Myfanwy set up home together, subsequently marrying in February 1937. Fired with enthusiasm, *Axis* was issued initially as a quarterly, but given its restricted subject matter and a subscription list of a mere two hundred, publication became more intermittent; the eighth and last issue was dated 'Early Winter 1937'. Piper was involved in the design and production, helping select the black-and-white illustrations and experimenting with cutting Paramat blocks, a method he had cribbed from the advertising world as an inexpensive method for adding occasional notes of colour. The blocks, as Piper described them 'consisted of a thin sheet of aluminium mounted by a thin sheet of rubber composition which could be cut away with a model-maker's knife to leave the area required in relief which could then be inked and printed.'[10] This was particularly effective with the reproduction of a painting by Miró as well as an example of his own work that accompanied an article by Herta Wescher in *Axis* 4. A further article in the same issue 'Piper and Abstract Possibilities' by Hugh Gordon Porteus is of particular interest in the light of Piper's subsequent work, as it could not have been printed without his prior approval.

Porteus wrote: 'Piper's paintings, reproduced here, show his attempts to escape from the mechanical trap. The results have a beauty, a purity an honesty which must compel admiration. Piper has made himself an absolute master of the game he plays. I should like to see him loosen the restrictions he still imposes on himself. I should like to see him explore the potentialities of linear rhythms, for example, as Wyndham Lewis has done.

'Wyndham Lewis is a visionary, and a visionary must burst the bounds of any game. Piper's is the proper procedure for anyone not *born* a visionary. His work shows a steady progress out of decoration into magic, the magic that occurs in spite of "pure form", or over and above his still-too-purified forms. His recent works are therefore equally important as contemporary phenomena and as example – as programme.'[11]

A decade later, and presumably recalling his innovative experiments with the Paramat blocks, Piper wrote: 'When a painter's work is reproduced in colour, by whatever method, he should ask for a lively parallel to his work, not for an imitation of it, in colour or any other particular. He should ask, in fact, for the same kind of result he would get if he translated a work of his own into another medium.'[12] He had done just that in *Axis*, as well as translating works by Picasso, Hélion, Nash, Miró and others.

January 1935

AXIS

A QUARTERLY REVIEW OF CONTEMPORARY
"ABSTRACT" PAINTING & SCULPTURE
Editor: Myfanwy Evans

● writers in this number

Herbert Read
Geoffrey Grigson
Anatole Jakovski
Paul Nash
H. S. Ede
Myfanwy Evans

● artists

Arp
Calder
Domela
Erni
Giacometti
Gonzalez
Hélion
Hepworth
Jackson
Kandinsky
Miró
Mondrian
Moore
Nash
Nicholson
Picasso
Piper
Richards
Wadsworth

1

two shillings and sixpence

AXIS 1, *January 1935, the editor Myfanwy Evans - later Mrs Piper - recruited internationally-renowned writers and artists to contribute to the magazine. The first six issues described as 'abstract' under the Axis masthead were in tentative inverted commas.*

Ben Nicholson, whose relief, *Painting*, 1935, he had enhanced in this manner for *Axis* 2, was outraged when he realised that Piper looked on abstraction merely as a useful tool or programme, but, as Porteus had opined, by the latter part of 1937, Piper was trying to escape the mechanical trap, and was shortly to produce not only the *Shell Guide to Oxon*, but *Brighton Aquatints*, arguably his finest series of topographical prints.

Once liberated from the self-imposed restrictions of geometric abstraction, Piper felt rejuvenated, darting around in all directions, making a film with Myfanwy for the B.B.C., designing his first stage sets, and writing articles on topics ranging from 'English Sea Pictures' to 'The Art of the Early Crosses'. The latter, for *Country Life*, picked up on a theme that he had first explored in a pioneering article a few years earlier in *Architectural Review* – one of the few general articles he wrote during his abstract years – in which he noted that the 'purely non-figurative artists of some of the early Northumbrian and Cornish crosses were the forbears of the pure abstractionists of today.'[13] In the same article, illustrated with his own photographs, he reproduced what he described as a 'Picasso-like profile' on the font at Morville in Shropshire, commenting that it could have had a comfortable place in the International Surrealist Exhibition. For those who remained intolerant abstractionists, like Nicholson, this change of direction was a betrayal, but for Piper it was pivotal and 1938 really marks the year of his maturity. He no longer had to justify his enthusiasm for mediaeval sculpture by comparing it to Picasso or the Surrealists, it, like Piper himself, could stand confidently on its own feet. He had also recently made two new friends who would play important rôles in the direction and variety of his work for the rest of his life: John Betjeman and Benjamin Britten. Betjeman, who met Piper through J.M. Richards, already a member of the editorial staff of *Architectural Review*, commissioned the *Shell Guide to Oxon*, while Britten composed the music for Stephen Spender's politically-charged play *Trial of a Judge*. Produced by the Group Theatre, it ran for ten days at the Unity Theatre, St Pancras, in March 1938.

Betjeman, who christened Myfanwy 'Goldilox' or 'Goldilegz', was soon writing witty and affectionate letters to both of them, addressing John as 'Mr Pahper' or, occasionally, 'Mr Pahpa', with comments on box pews, fluted columns, queer capitals and galleries, stimulating Piper's own enthusiasm for ancient churches and eighteenth-century non-conformist chapels. Over the years, they were to share many church-crawling expeditions, co-editing the *Murray Guides* to Buckinghamshire and Berkshire, and collaborating as author and artist on *First and Last Loves*, a delightful and idiosyncratic mini-survey of chapel architecture. Betjeman's text had originally appeared in *Architectural Review* in December 1940 accompanied by Piper's photographs, but when, twelve years later, John Murray republished the essay in book-form, Piper translated his photographic images into an individualistic mixture of pen, ink and collage, exploiting the textural qualities of marbled papers and sheet music to enhance the unique characteristics of each building.

Piper's distancing himself from the doctrinaire adherents of non-figuration may have had as much to do with politics as aesthetics. With his left-of-centre, but essentially open-minded and liberal approach to life and to art, he could not help but be acutely aware of the impending cataclysm, which was inevitably to lead to the destruction of so many things he held dear. Too old at thirty-seven on the outbreak of war to be eligible for conscription, he joined the Home Guard, as well as offering his services to the Central Air Photograph Interpretation Unit. He also involved himself with the 'Recording Britain' scheme financed by the Pilgrim Trust, and became the regular critic for the *Spectator*. His work with 'Recording Britain' led to him being approached by the War Artists Advisory Committee – chaired by his friend Kenneth Clark – and assigned to the Ministry of Information with a brief to record bomb-damaged buildings. By chance, he was in Northampton on 14th November 1940, the night Coventry was bombed, and was able to be in the city early the following morning while it was still burning. His two paintings of the ruins of St Michael's Cathedral painted that day, along with his *St Mary-le-Port, Bristol* are among the iconic images of World War Two.

Piper's commission to make a visual record of bombed buildings was a task ideally suited to his temperament and his growing fascination with the English nineteenth-century romantic painters. Blake, as we have seen, was an early inspiration, but under the influence of Geoffrey Grigson, a friend who had been one of

A Miro painting from AXIS 8, 1937. *From Paramat rubber composition blocks cut by Piper, adding colour to what was essentially a black and white publication and as a cost saving on making four-colour process blocks. For other reproductions of non-linear paintings, colour was added over black halftone blocks.*

the sponsors of *Axis*, he came increasingly to look at the work of Samuel Palmer, among others. In 1942, he published the volume on *British Romantic Painters* in Collins's popular *Britain in Pictures* series. That same year, he took the opportunity to mark the centenary of the death of John Sell Cotman with a celebratory article in *Architectural Review*, in which he wrote that 'The texture of a wall interested Cotman more than its solidity. There lies his strength as well as his weakness. He was much obsessed by death and decay in old buildings.'[14] Comments that could equally have applied to Piper's own work at the time, and are not so different from Myfanwy's defence of Picasso in the battle over abstraction five years previously in *The Painter's Object*. Here she noted that Picasso's 'whole practice as an artist has been to make a formal virtue out of chaos, to exploit the incredible ruin and inconsequence and purposelessness of the world today'.[15] As with *Axis*, Piper designed the cover for *The Painter's Object*: he listed the contributors' names in a column down the right-hand side, though using their signatures rather than type, and embellished the cover with one of his own photographs depicting a semaphore station wittily framed in an artist's palette like a large question mark.

Among the polymath Piper's many interests was lettering and typography, something that he had exploited in a modernist manner for the various covers of *Axis*. Yet, he was just as interested in carved letter-forms – taking rubbings from old tombs and inscriptions on his church perambulations – and photographing and collecting old sign boards and other examples of unsophisticated decorative signage and folk art; an interest that achieved popular acclaim in his poster designs for the Ealing Studios 1945 productions of *Painted Boats* and *Pink String and Sealing Wax*. Although there may have been a degree of friendly solidarity and support during those ration-stricken years, Osbert Lancaster singled out Ealing Studios for the 'advent of such artists as Piper, Ardizzone, Barnett Freedman and Bawden to the cinema hoardings', in an article praising Ealing Studios for adopting 'so radical a line in so conservative a sphere.'[16]

Like all the designers and architects of his generation, Piper's career was given an enormous boost by the Festival of Britain, for which he designed not only the great mural, *The Englishman's Home*, but also – in collaboration with Osbert Lancaster – devised the layout for the Festival Pleasure Gardens. *The Englishman's Home*, painted in Ripolin house-paint on 42 panels, decorated the exterior of the Homes and Gardens Pavilion; it is one of the few murals to have survived the politically-motivated over-hasty destruction of the site, instigated by the incoming Conservative Government immediately after the Festival's closure at the end of September 1951. Piper's mural is full of nostalgia, with echoes of his own earlier works, including *Brighton Aquatints*, *The Castles on the Ground* – J.M. Richards's 1946 book of suburban architecture – and *Buildings and Prospects*.

Until this time, apart from his abstract design for the set of *Trial of a Judge* and Frederick Ashton's 1943 ballet, *The Quest*, in which he developed ideas based on Inigo Jones's elaborate early 17th-century masques, his design work had been entirely graphic, but he was about to explode into one of the most diverse designers of his generation. Although much of this design work – particularly for the theatre, murals, mosaics, textiles and tapestries – was to remain graphics based, he was to enter into rewarding partnerships with Patrick Reyntiens, David Wasley and Joseph Nuttgens designing stained glass; with Geoffrey Eastop in ceramics; and, most explosively of all, with Ron Lancaster and John Deeker, for some of the greatest pyrotechnic displays that Britain has witnessed since the eighteenth-century.

As Frances Spalding says: 'If we knew nothing about Piper except his work for the stage he would still be an influential figure in the post-1945 period.'[17] Although there had been several abortive discussions concerning theatre design during the war years, apart from *The Quest* and Michel Saint-Denis's 1945 production of *Oedipus Rex* at the New Theatre, nothing had come of them. Indeed, the opera-world had to wait for the presentation of Benjamin Britten's new opera, *The Rape of Lucretia*, staged to celebrate the reopening of Glyndebourne in 1946, to witness Piper's genius for stage and costume design. Rationing of materials was still severe, but, fortunately, a cache of cream-coloured jersey silk was found for the costumes, which was dyed under Piper's direction by a team from the John Lewis Partnership. The sculptor, Willi Soukop, modelled the series of dancing figures that adorned the arcading in the hall of Lucretia's house, the second of Piper's two sets. Recalling the

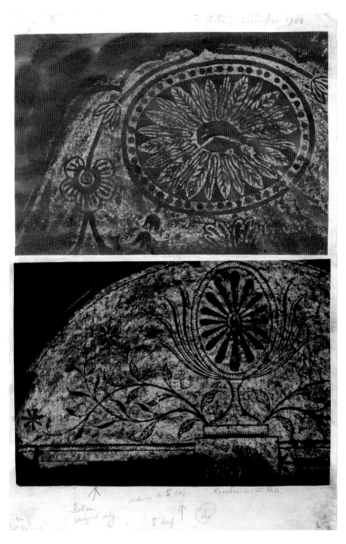

Piper made rubbings from gravestones throughout his working life and frequently used these, his own marble papers, and collaged printed pages to add texture to his prints and graphics.

event a few years later, Piper wrote: 'Composer, librettist (Ronald Duncan), producer (Eric Crozier) and designer discussed the whole production from the start. The general principles, the "manner", were indicated by Britten in the very beginning, though only in the most general terms… The settings were worked out in broad general terms by Eric Crozier and myself at an early stage on a half-inch scale model, that I made myself under his direction.'[18] The model was quickly acquired by Leigh Ashton for the Victoria & Albert Museum. As the set painting had to be done on sight at Glyndebourne, Piper stayed for the duration with Peggy Angus at Furlongs, the cottage near Lewes that, incidentally, Eric Ravilious had used for his love-trysts with Helen Binyon.

The Rape of Lucretia was the beginning of a rich and fruitful collaboration between Britten and Piper, continuing with a production of Albert Herring at Glyndebourne the following year, Billy Budd (1951) and Gloriana (1953) both at Covent Garden, The Turn of the Screw at La Fenice in Venice (1954), Owen Wingrave, for BBC Television (Commissioned: 1967; Broadcast: 1971) and Death in Venice for the Maltings at Snape in 1973. For the last three of these, Myfanwy Piper contributed the libretti. The 1950s was Piper's most productive decade in terms of the theatre, although he turned down a number of offers, insisting that he could not do more than one production a year. In addition to his collaboration with Britten, he produced set designs for the Royal Opera House's productions of Bizet's The Pearl Fishers in 1954 and for The Magic Flute the following year.

With rare exceptions, such as Inigo Jones's masques, Picasso's designs for The Three Cornered Hat, Lovat Fraser's for The Beggars' Opera and Cecil Beaton's Ascot set for My Fair Lady, theatre design is an essentially ephemeral affair, and those set and costume designs that are remembered are largely known through preliminary sketches and scale models. With The Rape of Lucretia, however, it is through the vibrant watercolours, several of which were done after the event, for the Bodley Head's lavish book of the opera, that the visual impact of this production has been perpetuated. In stark contrast to the ephemerality of 'stage art', stained glass is among the most enduring of all craft mediums, and it is not surprising that, with his long-time enthusiasm for English mediaeval glass, there would come a time when he would be asked to produce original designs of his own. This happened in 1953 when he was asked to submit designs for three three-light windows in the apse of Arthur Blomfield's 1920s Chapel at Oundle School. The narrow window-lights reminded Piper of the elongated niches on the West front of Chartres Cathedral with their attenuated 12th-century carvings, and in discussion with his old friend, the Reverend Victor Kenna, he decided to portray nine aspects of Christ – three to each window.

By happy chance, the Betjemans had recently met Patrick Reyntiens, one of the outstanding stained-glass practitioners of his generation, and introduced him to Piper, who gave him a working drawing of two crowned heads for Oundle and asked if he could translate it into stained glass. Six weeks later Reyntiens returned to Fawley Bottom, the Pipers' Oxfordshire home, precariously balancing his stained glass panel on his Vespa. Thus began another of Piper's rich collaborations. Commissions for Eton College Chapel, Coventry Cathedral and St. Andrews, Plymouth, followed in quick succession. In his 1968 book, *Stained Glass: art or anti-art*, he paid tribute to what he termed the 'artist-interpreter, double-harness, design-makers'; although Reyntiens was not an easy 'double-harness' partner, there is no doubt that the greatest of all Piper's windows was the fruit of this collaboration, namely the Baptistery Window in the re-risen Coventry Cathedral designed by Basil Spence. While the archaic windows at Oundle are seen to their best advantage on a summer's evening, the great non-figurative Coventry window is at its most perfect in the morning sunshine.

The Baptistery window was a major challenge for Piper and Reyntiens, especially as, due to financial restrictions, it came late in the rebuilding of the Cathedral and the physical structure was already in place. This structure – which measured 85 feet in height and 56 feet in width – was divided into 198 lights, provoking Piper to refer to it as the 'nutmeg grater'. Although Spence had approached Piper in 1955, it was not until March 1957 that formal negotiations were opened; during this interval an important event had occurred: the exhibition of American art at the Tate Gallery, including a major room devoted to abstract expressionism, which had affected the intellectual and aesthetic climate of Britain. This awareness permeated the Reconstruction Committee at Coventry and enabled Piper to suggest that the window might have to be more abstract than at first conceived; and, after a summer holiday in France, largely devoted to looking at contemporary stained glass by such masters as Léger, Marguerite Huré and Matisse, he was able to put his first totally abstract designs before the Committee. For the next few years, Piper and Reyntiens were in and out of each other's studios, which were only ten miles apart; ideas and suggestions flowed back and forth, with Piper producing cartoons for each light and Reyntiens making the modello that is now in the Victoria & Albert Museum. It was truly a joint production. While installation was in progress during the summer of 1961, Piper was also consulted over six sets of new vestments for the cathedral: given his experience in the theatre and a couple of earlier sallies into designing copes – one of which had toured America in a Smithsonian-sponsored exhibition of British Artist Craftsmen – he was happy to get involved.

In total, during the next thirty years, Piper designed over 60 stained-glass windows working in collaboration with either Patrick Reyntiens, David Wasley or Joseph Nuttgens, his style varying according to requirements from the totally non-figurative to the Palmeresque, Matisse-like and even Chagallesque: the latter, especially, after he had worked on the restoration of the church at Tudely in Kent, where, in 1967, the d'Avigdor-Goldsmid family had commissioned Chagall to design a commemorative east window.[19] Gouache and collage were Piper's preferred mediums for the production of cartoons as they gave him the flexibility and fluidity he desired, enabling him to work quickly and to make rapid changes as ideas evolved either in discussion with the patron, or as part of the on-going double-harness dialogue with his chosen collaborator. Two of these windows, particularly, must have evoked a mixture of poignancy and pleasure: the memorial windows to Benjamin Britten (1979) at Aldeburgh and John Betjeman (1986) at Farnborough near Wantage in Berkshire.

An important event for artists and manufacturers was the exhibition 'Painting into Textiles' at the Institute of Contemporary Arts in 1953. The exhibition, organised by *The Ambassador* magazine, founded by Piper's friends Hans and Elsbeth Juda for the promotion of British exports, concentrated on paintings rather than finished textiles,

Abstract Composition, *auto-lithograph, 1938, printed at Curwen Press for Contemporary Lithographs Limited. One of a series of prints primarily designed for sale to schools as economically produced originals.*

with the intention that manufacturers would then commission work. As Lesley Jackson notes, 'The two firms who responded most positively to the exhibition were Horrockses and David Whitehead.'[20] In addition to buying Piper's original art-work, *Foliate Head*, from the exhibition, thus establishing a relationship that was to last until the company closed in 1970, Whitehead bought designs by Henry Moore, William Scott and Eduardo Paolozzi, among others. *Foliate Head*, which stands out from Piper's more generally architectural-based textile designs such as *Blenheim Gates* and *Church Monuments, Exton* is also notable as being among the earliest appearances of a motif that was to obsess him for much of the rest of his life, recurring in print, stained glass, tapestry and pottery. Although Whitehead was to provide Piper's most fruitful incursion into the textile industry, it was not his first experience, as five years previously he had used the repeat-image of a mediaeval carving as the motif for his contribution to Ascher's pioneering collection of limited edition artist-designed headscarves.

Piper would have seen various carvings of the Green Man over the years, most particularly in the church at Kilpeck in Herefordshire, and in the cathedrals at Exeter and Christ Church, Oxford. However his obsession with 'foliate heads', as he referred to them, was stimulated by coming across a copy of C.J.P. Cave's book *Roof Bosses in Mediaeval Churches*, with its tele-photo images of carvings difficult to discern in detail with the naked eye. A number of these bosses feature pre-Christian imagery, particularly the figure of the Green Man, linked to the Greek god Dionysus; he is usually depicted disgorging vegetation and in Northern Europe is associated with regeneration, the first signs of spring following the long cold winter. When, in late 1953, Piper took a break from the Oundle School windows to work in Paris at the lithographic studios of Mourlot Frères, he produced two of his most remarkable prints – *Foliate Heads I and II* – in which he successfully married his love for English mediaeval carving with his life-long admiration for the work of Picasso. The latter he had already demonstrated in his 1936 *Abstract Composition*, printed by the Curwen Press for Contemporary Lithographs Ltd., the firm he set up that year in partnership with Robert Wellington and Oliver Simon. From the time of his earliest visits to Miles Marshall's printing works, the pervasive smell of printing ink never left him; he worked in

virtually every sort of medium available to the artist, producing
a body of well over 400 images in one technique or another –
woodcut, aquatint, lithography, etching and screenprint – in many
and varied combinations and permutations. The closest he got to
linocut, however, was cutting the Paramat blocks for *Axis*, leaving
the field clear for Edward Bawden and the practitioners of the
Grosvenor School.

In the wake of the Festival of Britain and Coventry Cathedral, Piper
was in demand for a wide range of design projects. The North
Thames Gas Board commissioned a mosaic for the outside wall of
their Fulham showroom, his abstract design for which was again
conceived in collage and translated this time into fibre-reinforced
coloured resin by David Gillespie and Tony Manzerolli; Manzerolli
worked with him later on the 29-foot-long enamel-like panel
for the Corn Exchange at Exeter. Having embarked on murals,
furnishing textiles and stained-glass windows it was inevitable
that tapestry commissions would follow. The first of these, in the
mid-1960s, came from Chichester Cathedral, where the patron
and collector Walter Hussey was now Dean. Piper had designed
a cope for Hussey, which had been presented to him on his
retirement from his previous incumbency in Northampton. The
idea for tapestry was obviously stimulated by Sutherland's *Christ in
Glory* at Coventry, but it was also the result of practical discussions
between Piper, Hussey and the Cathedral architect, Robert Potter,
concerning the sanctuary and siting of the high altar. The result
was not a tapestry in the conventional manner, but a sequence of
seven boldly-coloured, strip-like banners 15-feet high but only
3-feet wide. Ten years later, he designed a more conventional series
of tapestries for Hereford Cathedral, but in the meantime had
executed a number of other designs, both domestic and public,
including *The Five Gates of London*, woven by the Dovecot Studios
tapestry works in Edinburgh and the ubiquitous *Foliate Heads Tapestry*,
which was produced as a limited edition for the trade.

Piper had already had a kiln installed at Fawley Bottom before
he met Geoffrey Eastop in 1968, another of the craftsman-
collaborators with whom he was to work closely. Eastop had
worked previously at the Odney Pottery at Cookham and with
Alan Caiger-Smith at Aldermaston before being invited by Piper

Sample tapestry panel depicting the winged ox symbol for St. Luke, woven by Pinton Frères, for Chicester Cathedral, 1965.

to come and use the pottery studio on his days off from lecturing at the Berkshire College of Art and Design. The result, over the next few years, was a steady stream of slip-decorated thrown and press-moulded earthenware pots and large dishes. Later, Piper also worked for a brief time with the Fulham Pottery on a range of ornamental obelisks.

Piper the polymath painter and designer finally achieved a kind of apotheosis with an intermittent series of firework displays over water. For centuries, fireworks have inspired awe in the hearts and minds of land-bound mortals, while the 'firework master' – a veritable painter in the sky – was imbued with near magical powers. Ian Hunter, the impresario and revered director of the Edinburgh, Brighton and London Festivals, on viewing the Coventry Baptistery window divined an embryonic 'firework master' in Piper and commissioned him to produce a display for the 1965 Commonwealth Arts Festival. That display, to the accompaniment of Handel's 'Music for the Royal Fireworks', was held in London's Hyde Park with the Serpentine mirroring the effect. Hunter commissioned him again the following year for the first of his displays over the Thames; others were to follow: in 1977 for the Queen's Silver Jubilee, 1979 for the opening of the extension to the Tate Gallery, and again in 1987 for the opening of the Clore Gallery. By a nice turn of fate, Ron Lancaster, one of the two consultants with whom he collaborated, was an ordained minister of the church, while the other, John Deeker, was chairman of the firework manufacturers Pains Wessex Ltd.

John Piper died after a long illness on 28th June 1992. Suitably, the memorial party at Fawley Bottom some months later culminated in yet one more grand pyrotechnic display, a performance that was repeated five years later in tribute to Myfanwy. Fireworks may be transitory, but their effect, like the main body of Piper's work is enduring, although with characteristic modesty Piper claimed that all he was really trying to do was to pack as much and as many colours into the sky as possible.

Peyton Skipwith

1   *Architectural Review*, vol.106, no.633, Sept. 1949, p.178
2   Quoted Orde Levinson, *The Prints of John Piper: Quality and Experiment*, London, 2010, p.31
3   Richard Ingrams, *Piper's Places*, London, 1983, p.21
4   The date generally given for this tour is 1921, but May 1923 is more likely.
     See Frances Spalding, *John Piper: Myfanwy Piper: Lives in Art*, Oxford, 2009, p.15
5   Piper, 'Working With Printers', quoted Orde Levinson, op. cit., p.23
6   Quoted Spalding, op. cit., pp.368-9
7   Quoted Antony West, *John Piper*, London, 1979, p.49
8   The date of this dinner is often given as 1928, but Ede's diaries record it as taking
     place in 1934. See Orde Levinson, op. cit. p.30
9   Piper, *Stained Glass: art or anti-art*, London, 1968, p.19
10   Piper, 'Working with Printers', op. cit. p.23
11   *Axis 4*, p.16
12   'Book Illustration and the Painter-Artist', *Penrose Annual*, vol.49, 1949
13   *Architectural Review*, October 1936, p.158
14   *Architectural Review*, vol.92, p.11
15   Myfanwy Evans, *The Painter's Object*, 1937, p.9
16   *Architectural Review*, vol.105, p.88
17   Spalding, op. cit. p.272
18   Piper, 'The Design of Lucretia', Benjamin Britten, *The Rape of Lucretia*, London, 1948, p.69
19   Seven further windows were installed in the nave at Tudely in the late 1960s, and
     four more in the chancel some years later, to complete Chagall's decorative scheme
     for the church
20   Lesley Jackson, *Alastair Morton and Edinburgh Weavers*, London, 2012, p.206

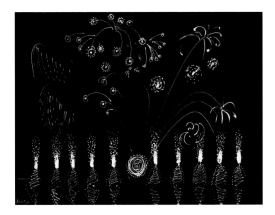

John Piper's design for the 1965 Commonwealth Arts Festival firework display.

WIND IN THE
TREES.

BY

JOHN PIPER,

With Decorations by the Author.

———

Privately Printed, 1923.

THE WINDMILL.

THE windmill, black and white,
Stretches its gaunt arms in lurid fright
Against the sky;
Where great grey massing clouds form beneath
white ones, floating high.

The sun slants through a cloud,
And the great hurtling wind comes, shouting loud
Across the tree-tops, far to near,
And rushes against the windmill, with its stark
arms, gaunt and sear. . . .
But the clothless sails wait; motionless.

8

THE GAUDY SAINT

AND OTHER POEMS

BY
JOHN PIPER

(WITH DECORATIONS BY
THE AUTHOR)

THE HORSESHOE PUBLISHING CO. LTD.
ST. LEONARD'S CHAMBERS
BRISTOL
1924

SIXTY-THREE: NOT OUT

A BOOK OF RECOLLECTIONS

BY
CHARLES A. PIPER

With Decorations by
John Piper

Privately Printed at
THE CURWEN PRESS
PLAISTOW
1925

*Wind in the Trees, 1923, The Gaudy Saint, 1924, and Sixty-three: Not Out,
subtitled 'a book of recollections' by Charles A. Piper, 1925, illustrated by his son.
Lovat Fraser's influence becomes less dominant by 1925.*

Marepond Farm, *wood engraving from* Leaves from Eden, *1929. The Royal College of Art magazine's foreword claimed 'the wood-engravings, which are mainly of rather fine technique, have lost much of the quality of a print taken by hand, chiefly due to the thick paper which has been used'.*

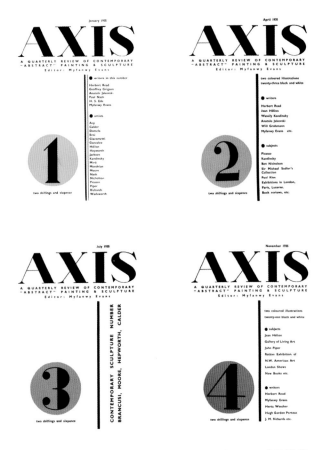

Piper designed the strikingly modernist covers for all eight issues of AXIS. The masthead lettering and issue numbers are hand-drawn, in the style of European magazine typography of the period.

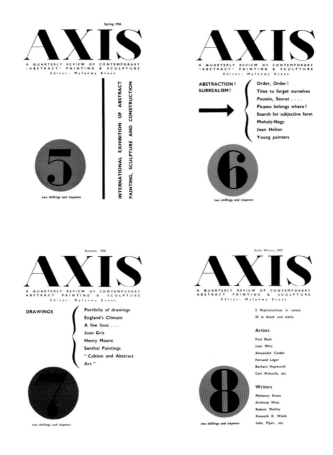

For what now seems a publication ahead of its time, it is not surprising that AXIS had a list of only 200 subscribers, and relied on donations to cover printing costs. The contributors were unpaid.

Abstract, *oil painting, 1935, owned by Hans Juda who, with his wife Elsbeth, ran the post-war textile magazine* The Ambassador. *The painting was used as a repeat pattern fabric in 1954 by David Whitehead Limited.*

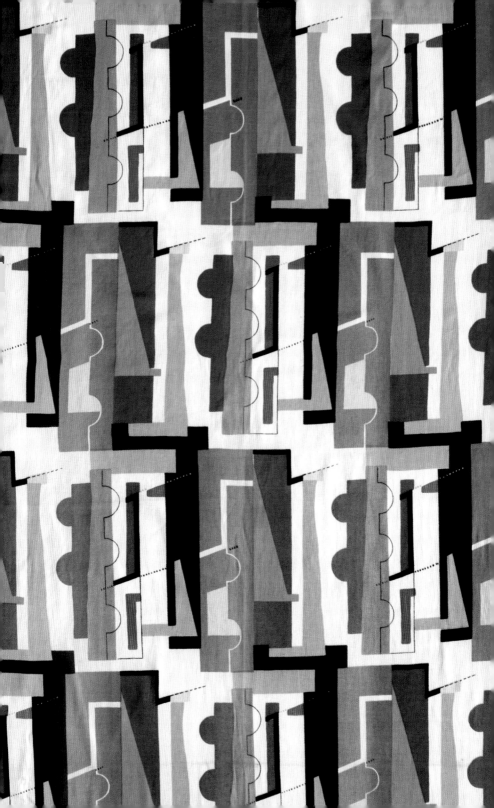

Modern Travel for Modern People, *booklet for Imperial Airways, 1937. Based on Piper's painting* Tall Forms on Dark Blue, *commissioned by H. Stuart Menzies of Stuart Advertising Agency, well known for using modernist images to promote up-to-the-minute products and services.*

Curwen Press, Newsletter 16, *1939, the cover of the company's house magazine illustrates the Curwen printworks in Plaistow.*

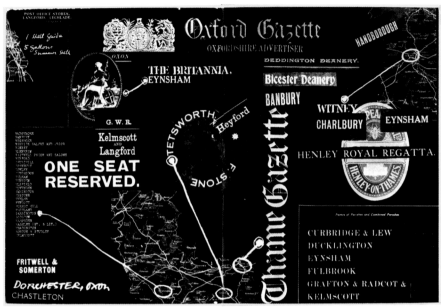

Piper – acknowledging John Betjeman and Paul Nash, whose Dorset
set the selective and idiosyncratic style for the Shell Guides –
wrote, photographed, illustrated and provided the collaged
endpapers for Oxon, *the Shell Guide to Oxfordshire,*
published by Batsford, 1938. Oxford is not included; as
Piper says in his introduction: 'This guide disclaims the
great city itself. Simply because there are only two
ways of treating Oxford: to overdo it or ignore it.'
The endpapers include a beer label, a local
newspaper masthead, annotated maps and his

receipt for five gallons of Summer Shell – Shell's
objective was to sell more petrol to car-owning
tourists. Piper co-wrote Shropshire, 1951
with John Betjeman, designing the covers and
endpapers, and commissioning Myfanwy to
contribute 'deserted places' to the guide. He
also provided illustrations and photographs for
Mid-Wales, 1960, using rubbings from 19th-
century gravestones. Piper later became editor
of the Shell Guide series in 1967.

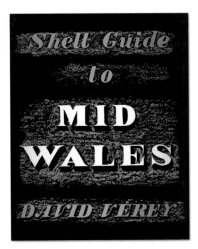

In 1938 Piper visited Ireland with John Betjeman, they returned with volumes of 18th- and 19th-century topographical prints. Piper's interest aroused, he enrolled on an aquatint course at the Royal College of Art.

Brighton Aquatints, *1939, corner of Bedford Square and Kings Road, Hove.*

Brighton Aquatints, *Regency Square*

John Betjeman introduced Piper to Lord Alfred Douglas who, reminiscing his youth, was pleased to write the introduction to Brighton Aquatints. *The twelve etchings and aquatints were printed by Alexander & Sons and the text by Curwen Press in an edition of 200 copies. A further 55 copies were hand coloured by Piper, with the exception of 'Brighton from the Station Yard', which was coloured by Betjeman. Piper conceived the book as an homage to early copperplate engravers.*

Brighton Aquatints, *The Royal Pavilion.*

Brighton Aquatints, *Bedford Square.*

Brighton Aquatints, *Regency Square from the West Pier.*

Brighton Aquatints, *The chapel of St. George, Kemp Town.*

Montpellier Spa 'Gothic', Portland Street St. James's, Suffolk Square Swiss, The Park St. Paul's (1831) Pittville Lawn London Road Bayshill Road

Continuing the theme of topographical illustration, Piper drew Cheltenham as a fold-out panorama, lithographed in three colours for Signature *13, 1940. The auto-lithograph (directly drawn on the printing plates by the artist) illustrated John Betjeman's article* Book Illustration Can Colour a Whole Town or City. *Piper re-arranged buildings and civic sculptures to emphasise the town's Italianate architecture discussed by Betjeman in his text.*

Pittville Spa
Neptune, The Promenade

Malvern Hills
Suffolk Square

Speculation

Italian, The Park

Christ Church (1837)

Signature, *like* AXIS, *could not afford to pay contributors, but the magazine which published 15 issues from 1935 to 1940, when Curwen was bombed, was one of the finest quality typographical and graphic arts magazines produced between the wars. Each issue included original prints by eminent artists and illustrators, a showpiece for them and the printer.* Signature New Series *continued a further 15 issues after the war.*

Piper arrived in Coventry on the 15th November 1940 the morning after the still burning Cathedral had been bombed. As well as Coventry Cathedral, he painted St. Mary-le-port, Redlands Park Congregational Church, The Temple Church, all in Bristol and St James, Waterloo Road, London as a part of Five Blitzed Churches, *a series of small sketchbook-sized gouache paintings.*

Cover designs and illustration, War Pictures by British Artists, Series One and Two, *1942-43. A total of eight small booklets published by Oxford University Press were produced, illustrating work by British war artists.*

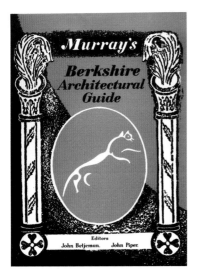

Murray's Guides, Buckinghamshire *1948*, Berkshire *1949 edited by John Betjeman and John Piper, and* Lancashire *1950, by Peter Fleetwood-Hesketh, who was originally commissioned by Betjeman to write the* Lancashire Shell Guide. *The series, published by John Murray, was intended to be more 'in depth' than the* Shell Guides, *but inevitably included some witty passages and Piper's photographs. Cover designs by John Piper.*

 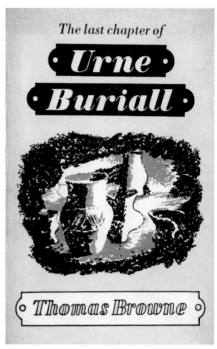

Poems in Wartime *by C. Day Lewis, 1940, published in an edition of 250 copies.
A classical bust with broken nose, is collaged into an emblematic black cloud,
symbolising the survival of culture in conflict.* Right: The Last Chapter of Urne
Buriall *by Sir Thomas Browne, 1946, printed and published by The Rampant Lions
Press, in an edition of 175 copies.*

Above, *Rievaulx Abbey*, top *and Park Place, Berkshire*, below. *Three-colour auto-lithographs from* English, Scottish and Welsh Landscape 1700-c.1860, *chosen by John Betjeman, published by Frederick Muller, 1944.* Opposite, *two-colour auto-lithograph, 'A Landscape from Within', from* The Castles on the Ground *by JM (Jim) Richards, published by The Architectural Press, 1946.*

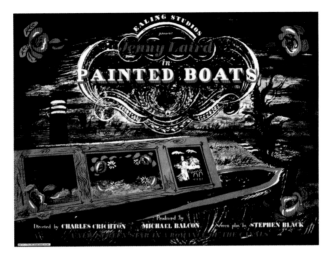

Film posters for Ealing Studios, 1945. Painted Boats, above, *includes traditional narrow boat painting and title lettering incorporated into a slate rubbing.* For Pink String and Sealing Wax, below, *Piper laid a photograph of the film's female lead, Googie Withers, over a 'Brighton Aquatints' regency terrace.*

The Traveller *by Walter de la Mare, published by Faber and Faber, 1946.*
For de la Mare's long philosophical poem, Piper produced four small paintings,
which were interpreted into lithographs in six colours by the master-lithographer
Thomas Griffits at the Baynard Press.

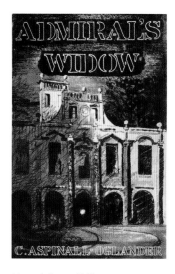

Hogarth Press, 1942.

Hamish Hamilton, 1945.

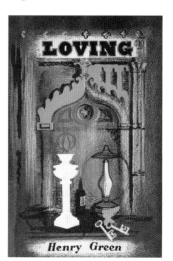

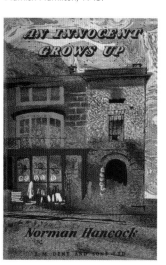

Hogarth Press, 1945.

J M Dent, 1947.

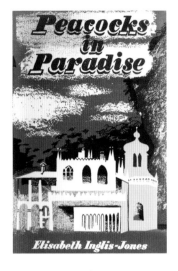

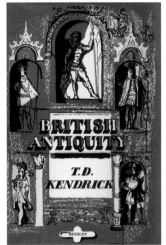

Faber and Faber, 1950.   *Methuen, 1950.*

Batsford, 1953.   *Faber and Faber, 1964.*

Set model for Benjamin Britten's The Rape of Lucretia, *1946. The three-dimensional model in painted card and wood was acquired by Leigh Ashton, the museum's director, for the the Victoria and Albert Museum.*

The Rape of Lucretia, *1946 and* Albert Herring, *1948, covers for the vocal scores of two of Britten operas. The cover design for* Albert Herring, *based on Woodbridge Town Hall, with collaged coat of arms, was used for the drop curtain.*

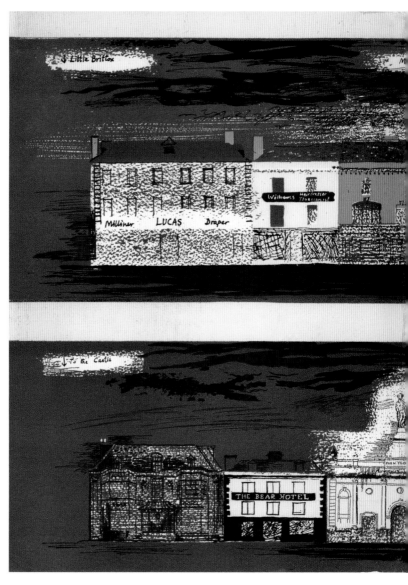

Buildings and Prospects *contains ten essays by Piper on British towns, illustrated with drawings and photographs, published by the Architectural Press, 1948. The dust jacket illustrates a walk around the market place of Devizes, Wiltshire.*

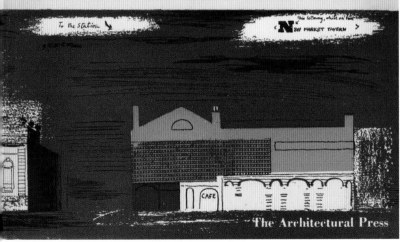

Image *magazine was the successor to the pre-war* Typography *and immediate post-war* Alphabet and Image *magazines, all edited by Robert Harling. The cover of* Image *No.2, 1949, incorporates Piper's slate rubbings, and his 1930s collages of Welsh chapels translated into lithographs, to illustrate John S. Woods' article 'John Piper as a topographical illustrator'.* Booton Church, *opposite, first accompanied 'Flint', a 1944 article in* The Architectural Review.

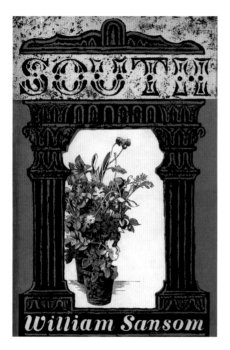

Piper used a variety of processes throughout his working life; South, *published by Hodder and Stoughton, 1948 combines collaged engravings and slate rubbings;* Romney Marsh, *published by King Penguin, 1950, has a marbled paper cover.*

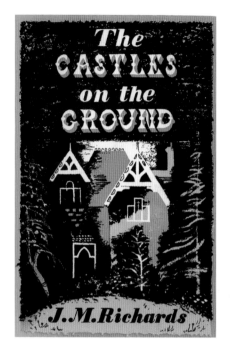

The Castles on the Ground, *1946, is illustrated with two-colour auto-lithographs and a three-coloured cover.* A Guide to Prehistoric England, *1960, is reproduced from line drawings. Below, rubbings of decorative letterings collected by Piper.*

Cover illustration for Scott-King's Modern Europe, *by Evelyn Waugh, published by Chapman and Hall, 1947.*

Two-colour illustration from On the Making of Gardens, *by Sir George Sitwell,*
The Dropmore Press, *1949.*

The Englishman's Home, *the largest surviving mural from the 1951 Festival of Britain, and the largest commission of Piper's career. Painted in Ripolin on 42 panels.*

Hugh Casson, Director of Architecture for the Festival described it as 'the one mural on the South Bank we can not afford to lose'.

Through John Betjeman and his wife Penelope, Piper met the stained glass artist Patrick Reyntiens in 1954. Piper had been commissioned by Oundle School to design windows for their chapel in celebration of the school's quatercentenary. Two Kings, adapted by Reyntiens as a trial panel from Piper's mixed media drawing, was the beginning of a collaborative partnership that lasted for 30 years.

The Street Scene, Gloriana, *lithograph, 1953. Benjamin Britten had been commissioned by the Royal Opera House to write an opera in celebration of the coronation of Queen Elizabeth II. Piper's Tudor sets and costumes were not a problem, but the opera's story and Britten's trying to reflect the economic and social difficulties went over the heads of the VIPs invited to the opening night.*

Fabrics for David Whitehead Limited, above, Figures from a Cretan Seal, *c.1954, the design of figures, symbols and creatures was taken directly from an early 1950s painting by Piper.* Opposite: Cotswold, *c.1960, relating to his ideas for stained glass, the design of* Cotswold *is abstracted to work as a textile.*

Marbled papers, vocal scores, pen and ink, typewriter, and positive and negative silhouettes create eighteen London churches for Faber & Faber's 1957 Christmas card.

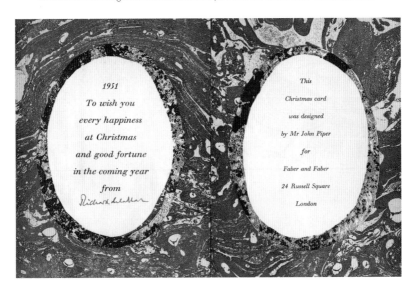

First and Last Loves, *by John Betjeman. Piper designed the cover and illustrations, again using pen, ink and collage for Betjeman's essay on non-conformist chapels, published by John Murray in 1952.*

Portland Stone: Portland Colours, *one of a series of articles written and illustrated by Piper for* The Ambassador, Number 6, 1954. *Edited and art directed by Hans and Elsbeth Juda, the magazine promoted exports by the British textile industry. Piper's illustrations interpret the effects of age and exposure on Portland stone.*

John Piper

Line drawing of the three three-light windows, The Way, The Life *and* The Truth *to illustrate a celebratory booklet* The John Piper Windows Executed for Oundle School Chapel by Patrick Reyntiens, *May 26th, 1956.*

*The Byzantine-influenced windows at Oundle, commissioned in 1953,
were Piper's earliest essays in stained glass, and his first collaboration
with Patrick Reyntiens.*

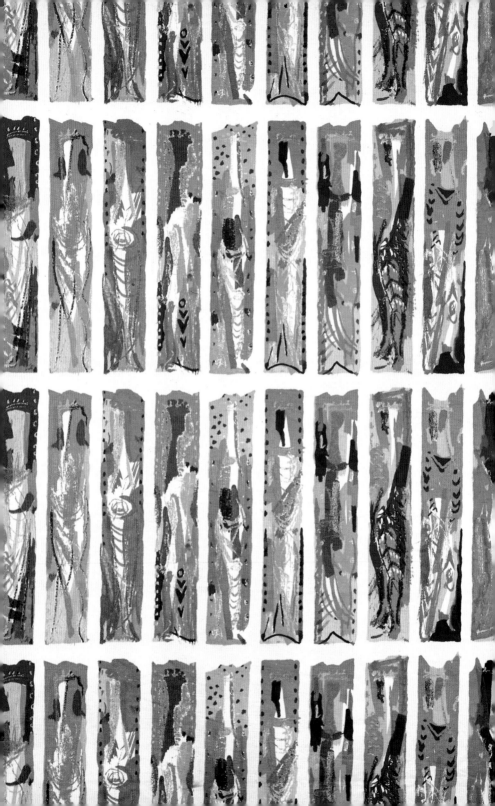

The textile and wallpaper company Arthur Sanderson & Co. commissioned Piper
to design a series of screen-printed cotton fabrics in 1960. Arundel, opposite,
was based on early figure drawings relating to the Oundle chapel windows.
Fawley, above, was printed in the early 1960s by David Whitehead Limited. The
fabric was named after John and Myfanwy Piper's home, Fawley Bottom.

For the Observer Film Exhibition, 1956, celebrating sixty years of cinema, Piper designed a full-sized shadow theatre. The 'shadow' souvenir, with characters (including a Betjemanesque silhouette) appear through a cut-out arch and behind a translucent paper screen.

John and Myfanwy Piper's friendship with Benjamin Britten (Myfanwy wrote the libretti for three Britten operas) led to a long-standing involvement with the Aldeburgh Festival, and the design of festival programmes for 1963, 1970, 1973, 1983.

A Century of Sanderson, *1860-1960, booklet cover, from the stained-glass panel design for the new Sanderson showroom in Berners Street, London, W1.*

Above, *four of many initial designs for a series of twenty-nine fibreglass panels, each twelve feet high and nine feet wide applied to the exterior of the North Thames Gas Board building in Fulham, London. Opposite, 'Ruins of St Mary Le Port', one of a set of four British Painting Royal Mail postage stamps, 1968.*

Coventry Cathedral, 1962. Trials for the baptistery window, above, and model, opposite, now in the Victoria and Albert Museum and watercolour design for vestment, right. Basil Spence's design for the rebuilt Cathedral was intended to achieve an integration of art and design standing beside the bombed remains of the old building, the ruins of which Piper had painted in November 1940. Spence's original plan for the baptistery window was to use plain glass, but after the critical acclaim of the Oundle windows, Piper and Reyntiens were commissioned to create their most challenging work, a window measuring 85 by 56 feet with wide concrete mullions. Piper spent nearly three years working on his designs. He recognised that his original plan for figurative designs for the window's 195 apertures would not work, and opted for an abstract solution of radiating colours creating an explosion of light.

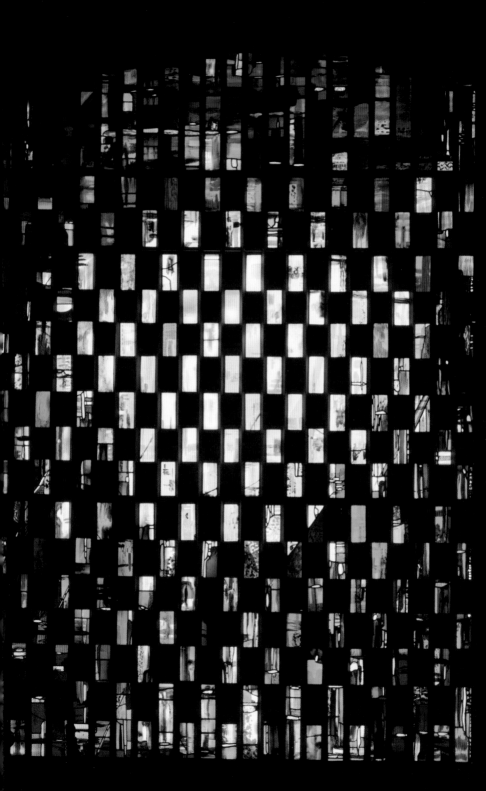

With help and guidance from the potter Geoffrey Eastop, Piper created a group of slip-decorated vases and dishes throughout the 1970s. These include the Janus-headed vase, above *and the* Castle Frome *plate,* opposite centre, *based on his photographs of the 12th-century Castle Frome font illustrated in the* Shell Guide to Herefordshire. *The 'yellow eye' plate,* opposite below, *dates from 1977.*

Throughout his life Piper derived inspiration from medieval stained glass, delighting in both its formality and the jewel-like quality of its colouring. He used this 1980 gouache of La Belle Verriere *at Chartres, left, to illustrate his essay* Stained Glass: Art or Anti-art. *Piper regularly worked out his designs for stained glass using a mixture of collage and paint, as in this full-scale design for* Christ in Majesty *for the Chapel of St John's Hospital, Lichfield, Staffordshire, 1984, right.*

The Light of the World *at Robinson College, Cambridge, 1977-78, with its effect of light flickering through cascading autumn leaves, is unlike any other of Piper and Reyntiens's windows. Working closely with the architect Isi Metzstein of Gillespie, Kidd & Coia, Piper, with possible reference back to the glass techniques of the Americans Louis Comfort Tiffany and John La Farge, created a sense of tranquility in quite an awkward space in this non-denominational college chapel.*

The Four Seasons, *1983,* top left: Spring, top right: Summer, bottom left: Autumn, bottom right: Winter. *Transfer-printed tiles 'from decorations by John Piper' were made at Fulham Pottery to be sold during Piper's Tate Gallery retrospective, celebrating his eightieth birthday.*

Queen Caroline's Monument, from the 1983 Hurtwood Press editions of Stowe, published in an edition of 300 copies. The book co-incided with the diamond jubilee of the school and the Tate Gallery's Piper restrospective.

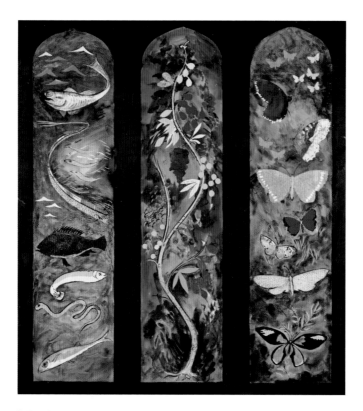

Full-scale mixed media design for the John Betjeman Memorial Window at Farnborough, Berkshire, 1986. Over the years Betjeman and Piper had visited many churches together, revelling in the detail and the iconography. For this exuberant memorial celebration of his friend, Piper has chosen a central Tree of Life flanked by fishes, symbolic of Christian belief, and butterflies, representing the resurrection of the soul.

Acknowledgements

Clarissa Lewis and John Piper Estate
Hugh Fowler-Wright
Nathaniel Hepburn
Simon Martin, Pallant House, Chichester
Patricia Jordan Evans, Bohun Gallery, Henley-on-Thames
Paul Liss, Liss Fine Art
Robert Upstone, The Fine Art Society
David Fraser-Jenkins
Brookie Fraser-Jenkins
Victoria & Albert Museum
Private Collections
Neil Jennings
Mr and Mrs Ian Beck
Robin Cox
Oundle School
Coventry Cathedral
Annamarie Stapleton

Photography
Textiles, Target Gallery
George Richards

Page 68, Two Kings, 1954, Mike Fear
Page 90, Christ in Majesty, 1984, Mike Fear
Page 90, La Belle Verriere, Chartres, 1980, private collection
Page 94, John Betjeman Memorial Window, 1986, Gordon Crabbe
Courtesy of Bohun Gallery, Henley-on-Thames

Overleaf: Romney Marsh, *1950, King Penguin.*

Be not
deceived evil
communications
corrupt good
manners
1. Cor. C.15.V.33.